IF YOU WANT TO
WALK ON WATER,
YOU'VE GOT TO
GET OUT
OF THE
BOAT

Books by John Ortberg

Everybody's Normal Till You Get to Know Them

If You Want to Walk on Water, You've Got to Get Out of the Boat

The Life You've Always Wanted

Love Beyond Reason

JOHN ORTBERG

with Stephen and Amanda Sorenson

IF YOU WANT TO WALK ON WATER, YOU'VE GOT TO GET OUT OF THE BOAT

ZONDERVAN™

GRAND RAPIDS, MICHIGAN 49530 USA

WILLOW

Willow Creek Resources

PARTICIPANT'S GUIDE | A 6-SESSION JOURNEY ON LEARNING TO TRUST GOD

ZONDERVAN™

If You Want to Walk on Water, You've Got to Get Out of the Boat Participant's Guide
Copyright © 2003 by John Ortberg

This title is also available as a Zondervan audio product.
Visit www.zondervan.com/audiopages for more information.

Requests for information should be addressed to:
Zondervan, *Grand Rapids, Michigan 49530*

ISBN 0-310-25056-0

Interior design by Susan Ambs

Printed in the United States of America

06 07 08 09 10 • 25 24 23 22

Contents

Preface

I want to invite you to go for a walk.

The Bible records many instances when God asked people to walk with him. There was the hard walk Abraham took with his son Isaac on the road to Moriah. The liberating walk Moses and the Israelites took through the Red Sea, followed by the frustrating, forty-year walk through the desert. And don't forget Joshua's triumphant walk around Jericho. Or the disciples' illuminating walk to Emmaus. The list goes on.

Perhaps the most unforgettable walk of all was Peter's walk when he stepped out of a boat one stormy night and walked on the water. When Peter went treading on the waves, I think he was experiencing walking at its finest.

Peter's walk stands as an invitation to everyone who, like him, wants to step out in faith and experience more of the power and presence of God. Water-walking is a picture of doing with God's help what we could never do on our own.

I believe there is some aspect of your life in which God is calling you to walk with and toward him. During these six sessions, you will learn the skills essential to water-walking: discerning God's call, transcending fear, risking faith, managing failure, and trusting God. When you are through, my hope is that you, like Peter, will accept God's invitation to go for a walk on the water.

—John Ortberg

What's Water-Walking?

There is something — Someone — inside us who tells us there is more to life than sitting in the boat. You were made for something more. . . . There is something inside you that wants to walk on the water — to leave the comfort of routine existence and abandon yourself to the high adventure of following God.

—John Ortberg

QUESTIONS TO THINK ABOUT

1. What kinds of things do you trust in, especially when life gets stormy, that help you feel comfortable and secure rather than fearful? Be honest!

2. Explain why you do or do not believe that God calls everyone who follows him to step out in faith and do something extraordinary. What does "stepping out in faith" look like?

3. How would you define failure?

4. Thus far in life, what has been your experience with failure ? What has failure kept you from doing? What has failure done for you?

VIDEO OBSERVATIONS

Images of a balloon ride

Following Jesus: choosing between comfort and growth

Did Peter fail—or succeed?

Discovering the power of Jesus

VIDEO HIGHLIGHTS

1. When John Ortberg and his wife took their hot-air balloon ride, the competence of their pilot became very important to them. Why is it so important for us to know the competence and trustworthiness of whoever pilots our lives?

2. Jesus invited Peter to step out of the boat and walk with him—to do something Peter could not do on his own—and Peter couldn't resist the opportunity. Jesus is still looking for people who love and trust him enough to step out of the boat. What do you find intriguing about stepping out of the boat?

3. What are your thoughts on John Ortberg's comments about failure, particularly that failure has more to do with the way we view the outcome of an event than what actually happened?

LARGE GROUP EXPLORATION

An Adventure in the Dark

Let's take a closer look at what happened when Jesus revealed himself to his disciples as they sailed across the stormy Sea of Galilee, because that event matters a great deal to us today. We too have the opportunity to walk with Jesus in places we wouldn't dream of going on our own. Like each of the disciples, we must choose how we will respond to God. Will we sit in the boat, like the eleven disciples? Or will we, like Peter, leave the security of the boat and give God the opportunity to use us in extraordinary ways?

1. When Jesus told the disciples to sail to the other side of the Sea of Galilee without him, they obeyed. But what happened as they sailed? (See Matthew 14:22–26; Mark 6:45–50.)

2. What did Jesus say to them, and why is this significant today? (See Matthew 14:27.)

3. From Peter's perspective, recap what happened after Jesus told the disciples who he was. What is significant about Peter's response to Jesus? (See Matthew 14:28–32.)

4. What impact did this event have on the disciples? (See Matthew 14:33; Mark 6:51.)

5. What impact do you think this event had on Peter?

Who Deserves the Credit?

It's not the critic who counts; not the man who points out how the strong man stumbles, or where the doer of deeds could have done better. The credit belongs to the man who is actually in the arena ... who, at best, knows in the end the triumph of great achievement, and who, at the worst, if he fails, at least fails while daring greatly. So that his place will never be with those cold timid souls who know neither victory nor defeat.

—Theodore Roosevelt

Highlights from the History of Water-Walking

For a very long time God has been in the business of inviting people to be water-walkers. Here are a few examples to consider:

Person	Water-Walking Invitation	The Result
Abraham	Sacrifice his son Isaac. (See Genesis 22.)	God honored Abraham's faith and provided a ram for the sacrifice.
Moses	Lead the Israelites out of Egypt, which meant crossing the Red Sea with the Egyptian army in hot pursuit. (See Exodus 3:7–10 and chapter 14.)	God parted the Red Sea, allowing the Israelites to cross on dry land, then drowned the Egyptian army.
Joshua	Lead the Israelites across the flooded Jordan River with the ark of the covenant carried by the priests at the front of the people. (See Joshua 3.)	As soon as the priests' feet touched the water of the Jordan River, it stopped flowing and the people crossed on dry land.
Joshua	Instead of going into battle, the Israelites were to march around the walled city of Jericho with the ark of the covenant for six days, then march around the city seven times on the seventh day and blow horns and shout when the trumpet sounded. (See Joshua 6.)	God made the wall of Jericho fall down so that the Israelites could over-take the city—the first key barrier to entering the Promised Land.

Twelve spies	Believe that despite the frightening obstacles in Canaan, God would be faithful to give the Israelites the Promised Land and all of its goodness. (See Numbers 13–14.)	Ten of them refused to believe God and his promises and perished in the wilderness.
Rich young ruler	Give up his material possessions and follow Jesus. (See Matthew 19:16–22.)	He refused and went away saddened. We do not know what took place in his life.

SMALL GROUP EXPLORATION

Topic A

Where Do We Place Our Trust When We Are Afraid?

God knows how fearful we are, and he sometimes uses uncomfortable, real-world challenges to cause us to choose where we will place our trust. John Ortberg explains it this way: "The decision to grow [spiritually] always involves a choice between risk and comfort. This means that to be a follower of Jesus you must renounce comfort as the ultimate value of your life." Let's explore what God says about fear and choosing where we place our trust.

1. What happens when we place our trust in "boats" of our own making instead of placing our trust in God? (See Psalm 49:1–13.)

2. What did David realize about finding security in God rather than in things? (See Psalm 20:6–7; 118:6–9.)

3. What do the following verses reveal about God?

   a. Psalm 18:1–3

    b. Psalm 56:3-4

    c. Jeremiah 17:7-8

4. What has God said to his people over and over again, and why do you think he repeated it? (See Genesis 15:1; 21:17; Joshua 8:1; Daniel 10:12.)

Topic B

What Happened When These People Got Out of Their Boats?

The Bible records the stories of many people who had to choose whether to trust God and step out in faith. Let's explore what happened to two men who, like Peter, decided to trust God and leave behind the security, comfort, and safety they had tried to provide for themselves.

Moses

1. What happened when Moses—the adopted son of the Pharaoh's daughter—took matters into his own hands

when he saw an Israelite being mistreated by an Egyptian? (See Exodus 2:10–15; 3:1.)

2. How did God appear to Moses, and what did he want Moses to do? (See Exodus 3:1–4, 9–10.)

3. How did Moses respond when God presented the invitation to step out of the boat? (See Exodus 3:11–13; 4:13.)

4. Finally Moses took the plunge and returned to Egypt to urge Pharaoh to let the Israelites go. What happened as a result of God's power and the shepherd's water-walking obedience? (See Exodus 12:31–37.)

Gideon

5. Where was Gideon trying to find comfort and safety when God approached him? (See Judges 6:11.)

6. Gideon was afraid to take the challenge the angel of the Lord presented to him. How did God respond to his fears? (See Judges 6:12–18; 7:9–15.)

7. How did God use this "insignificant" farmer who finally decided to obey and trust him? (See Judges 7:16–24.)

The Pluses of Water-Walking

It is the only way to real growth.

It is the way true faith develops.

It is the alternative to boredom and stagnation.

It is part of discovering and obeying our calling.

The water is where Jesus is!

GROUP DISCUSSION

1. Fear of failure is one reason many of us don't step out of the boat. Some people view Peter's walk on the water as a failure, but John Ortberg points out that there were eleven bigger failures sitting in the boat. In what ways does our perception of failure affect our willingness to start water-walking?

Think about It

Failure is not an event, but rather a *judgment* about an event. Failure is not something that happens to us or a label we attach to things. It is a way we think about outcomes.

— John Ortberg

2. How much does our view of God's character and competence influence the degree to which we are willing to trust him and, in faith, to accept his calling and take risks?

3. Would you agree that sometimes the "boats" we create – whatever gives us an illusion of control, whatever or whomever (besides God) we are tempted to put our trust in when life is stormy – might actually be more dangerous than water-walking with Jesus? Why or why not?

4. If we keep choosing not to step out of our boats, what happens to us? To people around us? To our relationship with God?

PERSONAL JOURNEY: TO DO NOW

1. In *If You Want to Walk on Water, You've Got to Get Out of the Boat,* John Ortberg writes, "I believe that there is some aspect of your life in which God is calling you to walk with and to him, and that when we say yes to his calling, it sets in motion a divine dynamic far beyond merely human power." In what ways might God be calling you to get out of your "boat" and step out in faith?

2. Usually anyone who begins water-walking has to face personal fear. What deep fears keep you from really walking with and obeying God, from stepping out in faith and with his help doing what you could never do on your own? List fears that are specific to the calling you wrote down for question 1.

3. Looking back on your life so far, when have you said no to God's call? When have you said yes? Why? What happened as a result of those choices?

4. Which small or large steps can you begin taking this week to get out of your boat a little each day?

PERSONAL JOURNEY:
TO DO ON YOUR OWN

You've learned a few basics about water-walking and have been encouraged to think about your choices, your boats, and the opportunity to water-walk. It's easy to seek comfort and create boats, isn't it? That's why so many people choose that path. But God is calling you, as he calls every believer, to put your faith in him and start getting out of your boat a little more each day.

Set aside some quiet time to think about the following questions. There are no right or wrong answers, and nobody needs to know your responses, unless you choose to discuss them with someone. What's important is that you take time to reflect on some issues that you explored today, issues that may cause you to become uncomfortable or even a bit angry – at yourself, God, or someone else. By their nature, some of the boats people create are pretty ugly and secretive. Remember, though, that God loves you just the way you are. Whenever you are willing to get out of the boat, he is ready to help you do things you could never accomplish on your own. One of the first steps in the process of water-walking is assessing honestly where you are right now – and where you want to be.

1. Look back on your life. When have you stepped up to the plate, to use a baseball analogy, and tried to hit the ball? When have you refused to get out of the dugout when your name was called? Why? How have those decisions influenced your life – for better or worse?

2. Are you excited about your relationship with God right now? Is it dynamic and growing, or pretty stale? Why? How might what you've learned about water-walking start making a difference in your relationship with God?

3. Do you think you are a risk taker or a comfort seeker? Why? Write out some ways in which you have taken risks in your walk with God and ways you have deliberately chosen to seek comfort rather than take the risk of what God was calling you to do.

4. Ask God to make your heart and mind open to what he wants to reveal to you through this study and to give you the courage to face whatever issues come up in the remaining sessions.

The Tragedy of the Unopened Gift

Whether I'm a five-talent, two-talent, or one-talent person is not what counts in the long run. . . . I must come to identify, cultivate, invest, prize, and enjoy the gifts that have been given to me.

—John Ortberg

QUESTIONS TO THINK ABOUT

1. Identify the most valuable, irreplaceable gifts you have received in your life.

   a. Consider whether those gifts seemed so precious to you that you were afraid to use them. Explain your response.

   b. Evaluate the risks of using such special gifts compared with not using them.

2. Which gifts do we tend to value most highly? In what ways do we minimize the value of other gifts in light of those we consider to be most valuable?

VIDEO OBSERVATIONS

Two ways to look at a gift, talent, or ability

Jesus tells a story of three servants

The Lord of the Gift

The Lord of the Settled Account

The Lord of the Reward

VIDEO HIGHLIGHTS

1. John Ortberg's story about his grandmother's unused china is a poignant illustration of the choice we each must make regarding the gift God has given us. How strongly do you believe that God has given each of us a gift, talent, or ability of immeasurable worth? What have you chosen to do with your gift?

2. What parallels do you see between Jesus' parable of the choices made by the three servants and how we choose to use our God-given gifts today?

3. What encouragement, caution, or hope for using your gifts do you gain by recognizing God as the Lord of the Gift, the Lord of the Settled Account, and the Lord of Reward?

LARGE GROUP EXPLORATION

The Opportunity of a Lifetime

As we saw in the video, Jesus shared a powerful parable about a CEO who gave each of three employees a great opportunity. He "entrusted his property to them," generously giving each of them a staggering sum of money to manage for him while he went on a trip. It was the opportunity of a lifetime—vocationally, organizationally, and financially! Let's see what the parable reveals about God and the opportunities he offers to us today.

1. How much money did the three servants receive, and what criteria did the CEO use in distributing it? (See Matthew 25:14–15.)

2. Given this opportunity to exercise initiative, test their marketplace skills and judgment, and perhaps gain more responsibility in the future, what did each of the servants do with the money? (See Matthew 25:16–18.)

3. How did the CEO respond to what his servants had done with his money when he returned home? (See Matthew 25:19–30.)

4. What insight does Matthew 25:25 reveal about why the wicked, lazy servant buried his talent?

5. When the CEO returned, he settled accounts with the three employees (Matthew 25:19).

   a. What does the Bible reveal about what will happen when Jesus returns? (See Matthew 25:31–34.)

   b. What do the following verses reveal about God's rewards, the wonderful things he has in store for Christians who are good stewards of whatever gifts, large or small, he has given them? (See Matthew 16:27; Ephesians 6:7–8.)

The Tragedy of the Unopened Gift

To sinful patterns of behavior that never get confronted and changed,
Abilities and gifts that never get cultivated and deployed —
Until weeks become months
And months turn into years,
And one day you're looking back on a life of
Deep, intimate, gut-wrenchingly honest conversations you never had;
Great bold prayers you never prayed,
Exhilarating risks you never took,
Sacrificial gifts you never offered,
Lives you never touched,
And you're sitting in a recliner with a shriveled soul,
And forgotten dreams, and you realize there was a world of desperate
    need,
And a great God calling you to be part of something bigger than
    yourself —
You see the person you could have become but did not;
You never followed your calling.
You never got out of the boat.

— Gregg Levoy

SMALL GROUP EXPLORATION

Using the Gifts God Has Given Us

In the video, John Ortberg explained how, after his grand-mother died, the family discovered a box of beautiful china that had been safely packed away, apparently saved for a special occasion that never came. Each piece had been given to his grandmother as a gift, but she never took the risk of using even one piece.

In a similar way, each of us has God-given gifts. Some of us are gifted in prominent ways that are celebrated; others of us have gifts that are overlooked or remain unseen. What matters is that each of us seeks to be a wise steward of the gifts we've been given.

1. What kinds of gifts does the Bible say God gives us?

   a. Romans 12:6; Ephesians 4:11–13

   b. John 10:28

   c. Luke 11:13

d. Deuteronomy 8:18; Psalm 136:25

e. John 14:27

2. God doesn't give us gifts simply for our personal benefit. First Peter 4:10–11 indicates that we are to use our gifts and abilities to serve and bring glory to God. Note what each of the following Scripture passages says about how we are to use God's gifts to us.

Our Gift	How We Are to Use It	Scripture
Our Minds		Romans 12:2; Philippians 4:8; Colossians 3:2
Our Bodies		Romans 6:12–13; 12:1; 1 Corinthians 6:19–20
Our Money		Proverbs 3:9; Luke 12:15; 14:28; James 2:14–18

3. What does John 15:3–8 reveal about God's partnership with us as we seek to use our gifts for him?

God Multiplies Our Gifts

The Bible is full of examples of how the Lord of the Gift uses even the smallest gifts of talents, resources, or love to make a huge difference. Consider the following examples.

The Giver of the Gift	The Gift	How God Used the Gift
The disciples (Matthew 14:13–21)	Five loaves, two fish	Fed five thousand men, plus women and children
Widow (Mark 12:41–44)	Two small coins	Used it to illustrate faithfulness in his service
The disciples (Matthew 4:18–22; 9:9)	Themselves—simple fishermen, a tax collector, etc.	Used the disciples to spread the love and truth of Jesus worldwide
Esther (Esther 4:12–16; 5:1–3; 8:1–2, 10–13)	Herself—willing to risk death by going before the king	Used Esther to save the Jews from destruction
Samuel's parents (1 Samuel 1:20–28)	Dedicated their son, Samuel, to the Lord	Used Samuel as a prophet, priest, and judge to influence the Israelites to follow God

GROUP DISCUSSION

1. Would you agree with John Ortberg that fear causes many people to bury the treasure God has given them? Explain your response.

2. What is the danger of comparing the gifts God has given to us to the gifts he has given other people, and what can we do about it?

3. What is the relationship between using the gifts God has given us and getting out of the boat?

PERSONAL JOURNEY: TO DO NOW

1. How do you feel about the gifts God has given you? Do you prize and appreciate what God has given you? Why or why not?

2. In what ways have you used the gifts God has given you? How do you feel about your stewardship of those gifts?

3. What are some of the reasons you have not used a gift God has given you?

4. If Jesus were to ask you, "What are you doing today with what I've given you?" how would you answer?

   a. In what areas of your life are you not realizing your potential? Why?

b. In what areas of your life might God want you to respond to him in a different way?

c. In what areas of your life might God want you to take action?

5. If you have a regret regarding what you have done with your gifts, what is it? What steps could you start taking today to turn things around, to step out of the boat and start using your gifts?

PERSONAL JOURNEY: TO DO ON YOUR OWN

During this session, we've started to explore the gifts God has given us and why we need to use them wisely. But our motivation to use our gifts should be more than a sense of obligation. God wants us to experience the adventure of stepping out of our boats and partnering with him to use our gifts for his glory. Set aside some time to do the following.

1. John Ortberg points out three reasons why people bury their gift: fear, comparison, and sloth. Consider your gift and what you have (or have not) done with it in light of each of these reasons. How has each contributed to your current status as a boat potato or water-walker?

My Gift	Fear	Comparison	Sloth

2. In *If You Want to Walk on Water, You've Got to Get Out of the Boat*, John Ortberg asks his readers to imagine the following scenario. Take some time to imagine yourself in this scenario, then consider the questions that follow.

Imagine that your life is over, and you are led to a small room. There are two chairs in the room, one for you and one for God (who gets a very large chair), and there's a VCR. God puts a tape into the machine. It has your name on it and is labeled *What Might Have Been.*

Imagine watching all that God might have done with your life if you had let him. Imagine seeing what he might have done with your financial resources if you had trusted him to be generous. Imagine seeing what he might have done with your giftedness if you had trusted him enough to be daring. Imagine what he might have done in your relationships if you had trusted him enough to be fully truthful and fully loving. Imagine what he might have done with your character, if you had dared to confess sin, acknowledge temptation, and pursue growth.

a. If you had to name the "one true thing" that you believe you were set on earth to do, what would it be?

b. On a scale of one to ten, with ten being the most growth, how much are you presently growing in the following areas: Vocationally? Relationally? Intellectually? Spiritually? What do your answers reveal?

c. If you were to die tomorrow, what would you want your epitaph to say?

    d. Which gift have you left unopened that you would like to give to God to redeem and use for his glory?

    e. What do you want to begin doing today in order to come as close as you can to realizing the full potential of what God intends for your life?

3. Ask God to reveal to you what gifts he wants you to use, and then step out in faith knowing that when God commands us to do something, he enables us to do it, just as he enabled Peter to walk on the water.

Find Your Calling
and Get Your Feet Wet!

If I am going to experience a greater measure of God's power in my life, it will usually . . . begin by my acting in faith — trusting God enough to take a step of obedience. Simply acknowledging information about his power is not enough. I have to get my feet wet.

—John Ortberg

QUESTIONS TO THINK ABOUT

1. What would cause you to take a step out of your comfort zone and risk getting your feet wet?

2. What do you see as the difference between a calling and a career?

3. How do we know when God is calling us to do something?

4. What impact do our personal knowledge and experience of God have on our faith in him and our willingness to water-walk?

VIDEO OBSERVATIONS

A mission from God

Water-walking: what it takes to do it

Discerning God's call

Identify gifts and limitations

Get feedback

Genuine passion

Prayer

An ordinary man named Bob

VIDEO HIGHLIGHTS

1. In what ways does Bob's story encourage and inspire you? Could you imagine anything like that happening if you stepped out of the boat? Explain your response.

2. Why is it important for each of us to discern God's calling *before* we step out of the boat? How do we go about doing that?

3. What is wrong with thinking that we simply need to conjure up more faith in God in order to be able to step out of the boat?

LARGE GROUP EXPLORATION

A Mission from God

How do you know if you're on a mission from God? In his book *If You Want to Walk on Water, You've Got to Get Out of the Boat,* John Ortberg writes, "It is possible for us to make courageous, high-risk decisions that are stupid." To avoid such potential disasters, let's look at several passages of Scripture that will help us understand the difference between identifying and responding to God's call and making foolish decisions that have nothing to do with what God wants us to do.

1. What do we learn about Peter from the following vignettes of his life?

   a. Luke 9:28–33

   b. John 18:1–11

   c. Mark 8:31–33

2. Read Matthew 14:25–28.

   a. When we compare how Peter responded to the above situations with how he responded to Jesus on the water, what do you notice?

   b. What does the conversation between Jesus and Peter reveal about water-walking?

3. The Bible doesn't record what the other disciples said or felt when they saw Peter walking on the water toward Jesus, but if you had been in that boat, how might you have felt? What might you have thought? What difference would that night have made in your life?

4. In *If You Want to Walk on Water, You've Got to Get Out of the Boat,* John Ortberg highlights four indicators that reveal when God is calling us to take a first step of faith. Next to each indicator, write down how it can help us know where God is calling us.

Indicator	How It Leads Us to Respond to God's Calling
1. Fear	
2. Frustration	
3. Compassion	
4. Prayer	

What Is God Doing?

Scripture makes it clear that God is at work in the world and that he wants us to be partners with him in accomplishing his purposes. So what does he actually *do?* Here are a few highlights:

- Psalm 104:10–32 describes some of the work God does to maintain life on earth.
- Psalm 121:1–5 tells us that God never sleeps. He is always watching over us and protecting us.
- 2 Chronicles 16:9 says that God works constantly to strengthen people who are fully committed to him.
- Isaiah 40:10–11 portrays God as a loving shepherd who faithfully tends his flock.

SMALL GROUP EXPLORATION

The First-Step Principle

We may know and hear amazing accounts of God's power and faithfulness, but information alone doesn't arm us with courageous faith. Hebrews 11:1 describes faith as "being sure of what we hope for and certain of what we do not see." Faith grows as we step out without knowing the outcome and discover that God is trustworthy, that with him the impossible becomes possible. So let's explore what John Ortberg calls the "First-Step Principle," which enables us to expand into an ever-widening spiritual comfort zone.

1. Over and over again, the Bible records that people had to trust God and take the first step of obedience to God's command in order to experience his faithfulness. Consider, for example, what happened to the following people.

   a. Naaman (See 2 Kings 5:1, 9–14.)

   b. Jonathan and his armor bearer (See 1 Samuel 14:14.)

   c. Bartimaeus (See Mark 10:46–52.)

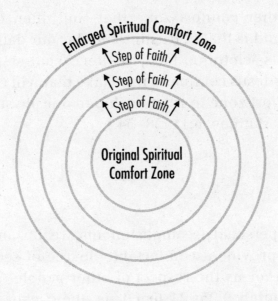

2. Just as the disciples in their storm-tossed boat had "spiritual comfort zones" in which they felt most comfortable trusting God, we also have spiritual comfort zones. John Ortberg says there is only one way to increase your spiritual comfort zone: "You will have to follow the Path of God, which requires taking a leap of faith. You need to get out of the boat a little every day."

   a. Peter obviously stretched his comfort zone when he stepped out of the boat. How would you describe the comfort zone of the disciples who stayed in the boat? (See Matthew 14:25–33.)

b. Another comfort zone that God often calls us to expand is that of trusting him for our daily physical needs – clothing, food, shelter. What steps of faith does Jesus command us to take that will expand our comfort zone in relationship to our physical needs? (See Matthew 6:11, 28–34.)

c. Our personal accomplishments, wealth, and strength can provide a comfortable degree of security and earn for us the respect of other people. What does Jeremiah 9:23–24 teach us about expanding this comfort zone?

d. Physical safety is another comfort zone we tend to guard closely. What step out of his comfort zone did God call Ananias to take in Acts 9:1–19?

The High Price of Saying Yes

Everyone in Scripture who said yes to their calling had to pay a high price. So will you and I.

Sometimes it will mean putting in hours of work and effort when you would rather not. Will you do it?

Maybe your calling will not involve the kind of recognition or wealth or influence you had always hoped for. Can you let that go?

Sometimes you will devote yourself to a dream — like Jeremiah — and things will not turn out the way you wanted, and you will experience crushing disappointment and discouragement. Can you persist?

Somewhere along the line, people will oppose you, disapprove of you, or block what you are trying to do. Can you endure?

Maybe it will take a long time to discern your calling. Maybe it will involve much trial and error and many false starts. And we tend to be impatient people, wanting immediate results. Will you be patient?

GROUP DISCUSSION

1. John Ortberg describes a calling as "something you discover, not something you choose." He goes on to explain, "The whole idea of a calling is taken from Scripture, where time after time God calls someone to do his work.... You and I are the call-ees and God is the Call-er. God equips the worker and assigns the work."

   We aren't used to thinking of our life's work in these terms, are we? Most of us have been raised to do our own thing in our own power. Let's talk about the adjustments we have to make in our thinking and actions if we are going to get out of the boat, get our feet wet, and live like people who are on a mission from God.

2. Sometimes we think we need to take a huge step out of the boat in order to fulfill our calling. But as we've seen in the video and in our study together, big steps are often the result of many smaller steps. In Bob's story, for example, he had no idea what would result from his simple step of daily prayer. So whether we have a big, long-term vision of God's calling for us, or see only the next step, let's share some of the ways in which each of us can step out of the boat a little more each day. Perhaps we can encourage one another to take the next step in following God's call.

3. Let's share some times when we vividly experienced God at work in and through us. What was challenging about following God's call? What happened that could have happened only with God's help? In what ways did the experience affect our faith?

PERSONAL JOURNEY: TO DO NOW

1. John Ortberg writes, "If I have the courage to acknowledge my limits and embrace them, I can experience enormous freedom. If I lack this courage, I will be imprisoned by them." What failures, fears, or limitations may be keeping you from getting out of the boat and discovering God's calling for your life?

2. Write out the activities you really enjoy, those that lift your spirit.

3. Considering your life so far, in what ways are you satisfied or dissatisfied that your gifts match your pursuits? What has your life so far revealed about the person God has made you to be?

4. What are you doing today as a result of stepping out in faith that you could not do apart from the power of God?

5. Who do you talk with regarding your desires, dreams, failures, and efforts to step out of the boat and pursue God's calling?

6. Try completing this sentence: I think my calling is ...

Personal Journey: To Do on Your Own

God longs for us to be in close relationship with him and to discover the calling he has for each of us. But discerning a calling involves great challenges of self-exploration and judgment. It requires ruthless honesty about gifts and limitations. It requires the willingness to ask tough questions and live with the answers. And it usually involves numerous attempts and failures. Yet there is no greater satisfaction than to fulfill our purpose in life and participate in God's great dream for the human race. Before the next session, set aside some time to consider the following.

1. Why is it important for each of us, in the words of the apostle Paul (Romans 12:3), to regard ourselves with "sober judgment," to accurately assess our passions, gifts, and limitations?

2. Read the table on the next page, which compares career with calling. Where are you placing most of your energies right now? Why?

Career	versus	Calling
Promises to give recognition, wealth, influence, and other positive benefits		Fulfilling God's calling may lead to difficulty and suffering, but it also gives us the opportunity to be used by God.
Often viewed as a means to a positive end—fulfilled dreams		Fulfilling God's calling may be disappointing, discouraging, and always requires deep faith. People may oppose us, disapprove of us, and block what we try to do.
Something we choose for ourselves		Something we receive from God
Something we do for ourselves		Something we do to serve God
May end with a comfortable retirement		Ends when we die
Provides temporal rewards		Significance of a calling lasts for eternity
Can be disrupted by events		Can, by God's enabling, be fulfilled despite the most oppositional circumstances
Often built on our reason and abilities		Is built on trust in God's faithfulness

3. If you don't feel that you are living out God's calling for your life, what steps might you take to begin exploring what his calling for your life may be?

4. What can you do to get to know God better so you find it easier to trust him and step out in faith?

5. As you consider the world around you, what need, area of the world, or group of people do you think God would have you pray for during the next six months?

Facing Our Challenges, Conquering Our Fears

It is hard enough to get out of the boat when the wind is calm and the water's smooth. But in life that is rarely the case. Sooner or later the storm strikes — in your marriage, work, ministry, finances, or health. It is in the act of facing the storm that you discover what lies inside you and decide what lies before you. . . . Storms have a way of teaching what nothing else can.

—John Ortberg

QUESTIONS TO THINK ABOUT

1. What are your expectations when you launch into a new adventure with God? What role do obstacles and challenges play in your walk with God?

2. What is God's most common command in the Bible?

3. What are the benefits of being fearful? In what ways is fear detrimental?

4. Do you believe that God deliberately asks us to do things that expose us to harm and can cause us to be afraid? If not, why not? If so, what is his purpose?

VIDEO OBSERVATIONS

The wind—and other distractions

Resilience in the face of trauma

God's command: "Don't be afraid."

When things don't turn out as we'd planned

VIDEO HIGHLIGHTS

1. In what ways can you relate to the experience of the Lewis and Clark expedition–expecting that the worst was over only to find out that an even greater challenge was just ahead? How do such situations affect your trust in God?

2. What are your observations regarding our vulnerability to temptation when our lives don't turn out as we had planned?

3. What three qualities did Joseph demonstrate through his life that are common to all people who not only survive but grow through difficult challenges?

LARGE GROUP EXPLORATION

Good News or Bad News, Keep on Walking

Many of us are familiar with the Old Testament story of Joseph, which reveals the ups and downs of a young man's life. Let's explore aspects of Joseph's story, taking note of how he kept choosing to walk with God no matter what storms came his way.

1. According to Genesis 37:3–11, what created division between seventeen-year-old Joseph and his brothers?

2. How did Joseph's brothers resolve their problem with him? (See Genesis 37:23–28, 31–34.)

3. Genesis 39:1–20 reveals what happened to Joseph following his arrival in Egypt.

   a. What positive things happened to Joseph?

b. What storm threatened to destroy everything Joseph had worked to accomplish?

4. Because of the lies of Potiphar's wife, Joseph was in prison for years. Genesis 39:20–41:14 reveals what happened to him during that time.

a. How do we know that Joseph continued to walk with God even while he was unjustly imprisoned? (See Genesis 39:20–23.)

b. In time, two of Pharaoh's officials – his baker and his cupbearer – were imprisoned and placed under Joseph's care. What did Joseph notice about them one day? What does this reveal about how Joseph was handling this storm in his life? (See Genesis 40:1–7.)

c. Both of the officials had dreams they did not understand. Because Joseph knew that interpretations of dreams come from God, he told the officials what their respective dreams meant. What did he ask the cupbearer in return, and what was the result? (See Genesis 40:9–15, 23.)

d. After the cupbearer was released, two years passed before he remembered Joseph. Imagine, for a moment, how you would have responded if you had been Joseph. How might these circumstances have affected your walk with God? Read Genesis 41:14–16, then describe the status of Joseph's walk with God.

The Resilience Factor

People who not only survive but grow through difficult situations have three qualities in common:

- They take action, seeking to reassert some command over their destiny rather than viewing themselves as helpless victims.
- They have a larger-than-usual capacity for what might be called moral courage — for refusing to betray their values.
- They find meaning and purpose in their suffering.

SMALL GROUP EXPLORATION

Choose Trust, Not Fear!

Let's look again at Peter's water-walking experience and then consider other passages of Scripture that will encourage us to choose to trust God and depend on him to lead us through life's storms.

1. When Peter first got out of the boat and saw the wind, he became afraid, started to sink, then cried out to Jesus to save him. How did Jesus respond to Peter's cry for help? (See Matthew 14:31.)

2. Most of us aren't literally stepping out of boats and walking on water during fierce storms, but we face other kinds of wind. What kinds of wind can cause us to become afraid, lose faith, and doubt?

3. In the Bible we find 366 commands from God not to be afraid. These are not empty, wishful-thinking commands; they are backed by the power, character, and love of God. What do the following verses reveal about choosing to trust God rather than fearing the challenges we face?

   a. Psalm 23:4

   b. Psalm 27:1

   c. Isaiah 43:1–4

   d. Hebrews 13:5–6

4. Many people whose stories are recorded in the Bible chose to take a step of faith and trusted God to be with them through difficult situations rather than to succumb to fear and give up. Read the following passages and describe how the individuals involved trusted God and took action in the face of great risks.

a. Daniel 1:1–15

b. Exodus 1:22–2:10

The High Price of Fear

Fear motivates us to take action and remove ourselves from whatever is threatening us. Fear readies our body to flee, hide, or fight. Fear can help protect us from harm. When fear rather than trust becomes our solution to difficult situations, however, fear exacts a devastatingly high price. Consider the following drawbacks of fear:

- Fear can strike when it is not helpful or wanted.
- Fear can be paralyzing instead of motivating.
- Fear can cease to be sporadic and become habitual worry.
- Fear threatens to keep us from trusting and obeying God.
- Fear that causes us to avoid a difficult situation instead of facing it head on and taking action kills personal growth. When we take the easy way out, we feel badly about ourselves because we learn that we can't cope with life's greatest challenges.
- Living in fear keeps us from experiencing our God-given potential.
- Living in fear destroys our joy and robs us of life's delights.
- Living in fear causes us to focus on the negative.
- Living in fear creates a loss of intimacy between us and other people. We become afraid to say what we think or feel, afraid of the pain of conflict.
- Living in fear causes us to believe that God can't, or won't, take care of us.
- Fear limits hopes, dreams, and callings.

GROUP DISCUSSION

1. Consider your life thus far and share times when God may have allowed you to face storms in order to teach you to step out of the boat and trust him. Describe what happened.

2. What else do you think God wants us to learn about him when things in life don't go as planned?

3. Joseph was resilient and found meaning and purpose in his life, even when the challenges just kept coming. What can we do to maintain our focus on God and keep on walking when storms engulf us?

4. John Ortberg writes, "Growth happens when you seek or exert control where you are able to rather than giving up in difficult circumstances. It happens when you decide to be wholly faithful in a situation that you do not like and cannot understand. It happens when you keep walking even though you see the wind. Then you discover that, somehow, you are not alone. As he was with Joseph, the Lord is also with you."

What encouragement does this offer you? Why?

PERSONAL JOURNEY: TO DO NOW

1. Have difficult storms in your life caused you to become more resilient, or more fearful?

   a. What has been the result of your resilience or fear?

   b. In what ways are you satisfied or dissatisfied with that result?

2. When you are confronted by threatening storms, what kind of temptations do you face?

   a. In what areas are you most vulnerable to temptation?

   b. How do you respond to those temptations?

3. Identify the areas in which you would like to step out in faith and trust God. What steps might you begin taking to accomplish this?

4. What benefits might you receive if you, like John Ortberg on his horseback ride, were to step out of your comfort zone?

PERSONAL JOURNEY:
TO DO ON YOUR OWN

God longs for us to trust him, to water-walk in faith and grow to love him more. He wants to replace our fear with faith. But if he is to work effectively in our lives, we have to face our fears honestly. Set aside some time to do the following exercises.

1. Rate your normal response to the storms of life on this trust-fear continuum:

Trust   **Fear**

2. In what ways has fear limited your growth in relationship to God? In relationship to other aspects of life?

3. Think about who God is and how he has revealed himself to you in the past. How does what you have experienced with him already help you step out of the boat?

4. List anything in your life that causes you to feel fearful and describe the ways in which that fear has affected your life. Then identify steps you can take to begin trusting God more and to start water-walking.

What I Fear	How That Fear Has Affected My Life	Steps of Trust I Can Take

5. Choose one of the fears you have described above and take the chance to "feel the fear and do it anyway."

Good News for Cave Dwellers

Sometimes you are in a cave and no human action is able to get you out. There is something you can't fix, can't heal, or can't escape, and all you can do is trust God. Finding ultimate refuge in God means you become so immersed in his presence, so convinced of his goodness, so devoted to his lordship that you find even the cave is a perfectly safe place to be because he is there with you.

—John Ortberg

QUESTIONS TO THINK ABOUT

1. Compared with toddlers, who don't seem to mind failure—such as being misunderstood as they learn to talk, and falling and bumping into things as they learn to walk—how do adults tend to view failure?

2. When people experience failure in their lives, how do they typically respond?

3. What aspect of failure is most difficult for you?

4. What enables you to move beyond a failure?

VIDEO OBSERVATIONS

To boldly go where no one has gone before

Responses to failure

David and the cave of failure

Good news for cave dwellers

VIDEO HIGHLIGHTS

1. Many Christians avoid talking about failure or times of "being in the cave." John Ortberg spoke frankly about dealing with failure and what God wants to accomplish in us when we're in the cave. What did he say that was new to you or surprised you?

2. What effect does the common response of withdrawing or protecting ourselves from failure have on our ability to keep growing and risking?

3. What is it about being in the cave that allows God to do some of his best work there?

4. When we are living in the cave, what does taking action accomplish? What makes it difficult for us to take action?

LARGE GROUP EXPLORATION

David's Experience in the Cave

There are many parallels between the life of David, one of the most adventurous men who ever lived, and our lives today. At first, as the Bible records in 1 Samuel 16:1–18:7, it seemed everything David touched worked out well:

- In the presence of his brothers and father, David was anointed by Samuel to become the next king of Israel.

- As a youthful shepherd, David volunteered to fight Goliath, a huge warrior who challenged not only the Israelites but God himself, and David succeeded.

- David was given a high rank in the army because he successfully did everything King Saul sent him to do. He was viewed as a hero who had done mightier deeds than King Saul.

But then events in David's life changed dramatically. Let's see what happened.

1. After experiencing a string of personal successes, David experienced a series of devastating losses. Read the following Scripture passages and write down some of the losses David faced.

Scripture	David's Losses
1 Samuel 18:8–11; 19:1–3, 8–13, 18–20; 20:1; 25:1	
1 Samuel 19:1–3; 20:30–42; 31:1–3	
1 Samuel 21:10–15	
1 Samuel 22:1–2	
1 Samuel 23:19–29	

2. Describe the relationship David had with God when all was going well in his life. (See 1 Samuel 17:32–37; 18:12–14.)

3. After facing the losses and difficulties outlined in question 1 (which are far from complete), how did David respond toward God? (See 1 Samuel 30:3–6.)

4. It's not easy to face the pain and discouragement of failure and adversity. There were times in David's life when he felt utterly destroyed. His response to one of those times is found in Psalm 142, "A *maskil* of David. When he was in the cave. A prayer." Let's look at this psalm, which reveals the cry of David's heart, and see how he faced his situation and found a way to go on.

   a. What do we learn from Psalm 142:1–2 about David's communication with God?

   b. In the first part of verse 3, what did David affirm about God?

c. In verses 4–6, how did David describe his situation? What did he count on God to do for him? Is it any different for us when we are in the cave?

d. What was David's hope and request in verse 7?

Did You Know?

According to Old Testament scholars, the book of Psalms contains different kinds of psalms: psalms of thanksgiving, psalms of wisdom, psalms about enthronement concerning the king, and so on. But the most common category is the psalm of lament. The most frequent psalms are those of complaint to God!

SMALL GROUP EXPLORATION

Point to Ponder

Optimism requires a belief that things will in fact get better for you and me. Hope includes the psychological advantages of optimism but is rooted in something deeper. When we hope, we believe that God is at work to redeem all things *regardless of how things happen to be turning out for us today.*

— John Ortberg

God: Our Refuge and Hope

We can't fix, heal, or escape all of our bad situations. Relationships fall apart. Marriages fail. Children disappoint. Illnesses debilitate. Jobs terminate. Our deepest dreams and desires remain unfulfilled. The list could go on and on. So sometimes there's no way out of the cave; we will be there for a while. But during those times, we can find refuge and hope in God. He understands storms and cave-dwelling firsthand. He is the God of encouragement. He is the God of power who never ceases to redeem all things. So let's investigate a few highlights from Scripture that reveal the hope God offers.

1. The following Scripture passages give us a basis for placing our hope in God.

   a. What about God gives us reason to hope? (See Psalm 62:5–8.)

b. What aspect of God's eternal character gives us reason to hope? (See Psalm 89:1–2.)

c. What do Philippians 3:12–14; 4:13 emphasize?

2. Hope got Peter out of the boat. Trust in God held Peter up as he walked on the water. Then fear conquered him; he shifted his attention from Jesus to the storm and began to sink. Peter's ability to water-walk hinged on whether he focused on the Savior or on the storm. Let's consider what God says about keeping our eyes focused on him so that we can gain hope in the midst of our most desperate situations.

a. Isaiah 26:3 and Romans 12:2 give us essential instruction regarding how we need to use our minds. What do these passages teach about where we focus our minds?

b. In *If You Want to Walk on Water, You've Got to Get Out of the Boat,* John Ortberg emphasizes that our ability to live in hope—to remain focused on Christ during the storm—is largely dependent on what we feed our minds. How and with what does God want us to feed our minds? And what are we to do with what we have learned? (See Philippians 4:8–9.)

c. In Psalm 119, the psalmist wells up with love for the Scriptures. Read verses 11 and 97–104 and explain why it is so important to meditate on Scripture.

Jesus Really Understands

Jesus, the Son of David, experienced challenging, painful losses while living on earth. In fact, many of his losses parallel David's losses, and our losses as well. Note some of the ways in which Jesus had firsthand experience with the types of losses we suffer.

David Suffered Losses	Jesus Suffered Losses
Was heralded as a brave, courageous, successful man (1 Samuel 18:6–8, 12–16) and loved by many people. Then he was forced to flee for his life from Saul (1 Samuel 19:18).	Was in heaven, at the right hand of God the Father, honored by the heavenly hosts. But because of the need to redeem humankind, Jesus came to earth as a human being (Philippians 2:5–11).
David was no doubt hungry and thirsty when he lived in the desert wilderness (1 Samuel 23:14–15).	Jesus was hungry after fasting in the wilderness for forty days (Matthew 4:1–2).
David's life was threatened numerous times (1 Samuel 18:10–11; 19:9–16).	People threatened Jesus and wanted to kill him (Mark 3:6; Luke 19:47).
For years David moved from place to place, not having a real home (1 Samuel 19:18; 20:1; 21:10; 27:4).	Jesus traveled from place to place, without a real home in which to lay his head (Matthew 8:20).
David's best friend, Jonathan, was killed (1 Samuel 31:2).	Jesus' beloved friend, John the Baptist, was killed (Matthew 14:6–11).
David's friends wanted to stone him after the Amalekites' raid (1 Samuel 30:1–6).	Jesus' best friends deserted him in the Garden of Gethsemane (Matthew 26:55–56).
David experienced great distress in a cave (Psalm 142).	After his crucifixion, Jesus lay in a cave until he conquered death and arose (Matthew 28:1–7).

GROUP DISCUSSION

1. In his book *If You Want to Walk on Water, You've Got to Get Out of the Boat,* John Ortberg writes, "In any arena where you are concerned about failure, the single most destructive thing you can do is *nothing.*" What does doing nothing lead to?

2. John Ortberg goes on to write, "We can survive the loss of an extraordinary number of things, but no one can outlive hope. When it is gone, we are done. Therefore the capacity to stay focused on the presence and power of God in our lives becomes supremely important." In what ways have you found this to be true in your life or the life of someone close to you?

3. What steps can we take that will help us cultivate more hope in Christ?

4. John Ortberg tells a story about a Christian woman who wanted to be buried with a fork in her hand because she wanted everyone to know that the best was yet to come. No matter how deep or dark the cave in which we find ourselves, God is with us. If we will focus on him and take the next step, and then the next, we can rest assured that something better is coming. For those of us who are willing, take a moment to share with the group the "something better" that encourages you.

PERSONAL JOURNEY: TO DO NOW

1. In general, how do you respond to God when you are in the cave of failure, pain, and disappointment?

  a. In what ways might your fear of failure hold you back from taking action during those times?

  b. In what ways might your view of God hold you back from taking action during those times?

2. In what ways is your sense of value and significance tied to your earthly success? In what ways is it tied to the fact that God loves and values you even when you fall flat on your face?

3. In what areas of your life are you in the cave? Identify several steps you can take toward trusting God in this area:

a. How honest are you being with God?

b. What do you need to do to adjust your focus on God?

c. For what does God want you to trust him right now?

d. What action might God want you to take to make positive changes in your situation?

e. What hard questions might God want you to ask?

PERSONAL JOURNEY:
TO DO ON YOUR OWN

God longs for us to trust him, walk with him, and grow to love him more. But we don't grow in these ways unless we make an effort to do so. Set aside some time to answer the following questions and do the following exercises:

1. What we feed our minds is important. Write down the sources of food that nurture your hope in God. Then write down the sources that tend to keep you in the cave, that feed your doubt, pain, or discouragement.

2. If you were sitting across from Jesus in a restaurant, what would he say about the things on which you tend to focus your thoughts?

3. List several positive changes you could make in order to focus more on Jesus. Be sure to include events that have revealed God's love and presence in your life. Feast on this encouragement!

4. Pray every day about a challenging area of your life—or that of a close friend or family member.

Learning to Wait on Our Big God

When human beings get out of the boat, they are never quite the same. . . . Every time you walk on the water, each time you trust God and seek to discern and obey his calling on your life, your God will get bigger, and your worship will grow deeper, richer, and stronger.

—John Ortberg

QUESTIONS TO THINK ABOUT

1. When in your life has God seemed unbelievably big to you? What impact has this experience had on your life?

2. How do you feel when you have asked God to help meet a particular need, yet your situation doesn't seem to improve over time? (Maybe it even gets worse!)

3. What do you think it means to wait on the Lord? In what ways does our fast-paced, horn-honking, express-line lifestyle make waiting difficult?

4. In what areas of your life do you find it particularly hard to patiently wait on God for his answer or action? Why?

VIDEO OBSERVATIONS

What keeps us from getting out of the boat?

How big is your God?

God gives us strength to walk with him (Isaiah 40:29–31)

God is always watching, protecting, and asking, "Will you trust me and get out of the boat?"

VIDEO HIGHLIGHTS

1. What kinds of things can keep us from fully trusting God?

2. Why, as John Ortberg explains, does Christ get "bigger" the more we trust him?

3. If we really believe that God is always with us, backing us up in the midst of our difficulties (even when we have to wait), how does that belief change the way we live?

LARGE GROUP EXPLORATION

How Big Is Your God?

John Ortberg writes, "I strongly believe that the way we live is a consequence of the size of our God." Our God is too small. We are not convinced that we are absolutely safe in the hands of a fully competent, all-knowing, ever-present God. That is why so many of us keep living as if everything depends on us.

In light of our tendency to live with the consequences of a small God, let's explore some Scripture passages that will open our eyes to the wonder of our great, big God.

1. What does Scripture say to those of us who live in fear and anxiety because we think everything depends on us? (See Matthew 6:25–34; 1 Peter 5:7.)

2. What does Scripture say to those of us who shrink back from boldly stepping out of the boat because we feel inadequate? (See 2 Corinthians 12:9–10; Philippians 4:13.)

3. What does Scripture say to those of us who believe our financial security depends on us? (See 2 Corinthians 9:8–11; 1 Timothy 6:17.)

4. What does Ephesians 3:14–21 reveal about how much God loves us?

5. How do we know our big, giant God cares enough to watch out for us and will act on our behalf when we are hurting? (See Psalm 9:10; 1 John 5:14–15.)

6. Job, who went through great trials that severely tested his faith, maintained an amazing trust in God. Despite what had happened to him, and his desire to question God, Job's God did not shrink. What was Job's response when God actually showed up and Job, who already knew God was big, saw God as he had never seen him before? (See Job 42:1–6.)

Worship in Perspective

Worship is a word for the process by which we come to perceive and declare the vastness, worthiness, and strength of God. John Ortberg explains worship this way: "Worship is not about filling God's unmet ego needs. God has made us so that when we experience something transcendentally great, we have a need to praise it. . . . We worship God not so much because he needs it, but because *we* do." In other words, worship is a recognition that God is "sooo big!"

So why is it important to worship God?

- Without worship, we forget that we have a big God beside us and live in fear.
- Without worship, we forget God's calling and begin to live in a spirit of self-reliance and stubborn independence.
- Without worship, we lose our sense of wonder and gratitude to God. We plod through life with blinders on, unaware of God's work in our lives.
- Our understanding of God grows as we reflect on what God has done and respond in worship.

SMALL GROUP EXPLORATION

Waiting on God

Just because we step out of the boat doesn't mean we'll immediately have smooth sailing. Sometimes we have to wait, and sometimes we have to wait through a storm in the dark. During the waiting, it's more important than ever to keep our eyes focused on our great, big God. So let's quickly review what Scripture says about waiting on God.

1. No matter how long we have to wait, what reason does Hebrews 10:23 give us for hope?

2. When we are waiting on God—obeying him but not yet seeing the results we hope for—Isaiah 40:27–31 reminds us of our hope.

   a. When we wait on the Lord, what will he give us?

   b. What does this passage reveal about the different seasons we will experience during our spiritual walk?

3. Waiting on God isn't just sitting around and doing nothing. God is always accomplishing something significant while we wait, so what we do while we wait is important. Note what the following Scripture passages reveal about how we are to wait and what we are to do while waiting.

Scripture	While We Wait . . .
Psalm 22:1–5	
Psalm 37:7	
Romans 8:23–25	
Isaiah 26:3	
Philippians 1:6	

Think about It

What God does in us while we wait is as important as what it is we are waiting for. . . . Waiting is not just something we have to do while we get what we want. It is part of the process of becoming what God wants us to be.

— John Ortberg

It's All a Matter of Timing!

It is particularly difficult for us to step out in faith and *wait* on God. Yet waiting is part of what God wants us to do.

In the story of Jesus and his disciples in the boat (Matthew 14:22–33), some of Jesus' actions were decisive and *immediate*. For example, he immediately answered the disciples' fearful cries and immediately saved Peter from drowning. At other times, Jesus *waited*. He waited until "the fourth watch of the night" — after 3:00 in the morning — before coming to the disciples on the stormy sea. Meanwhile, the disciples had been in the boat since before sundown. We can almost hear their thoughts as they fought to stay afloat: *Where is Jesus? Has he abandoned us? Doesn't he care about us out here?*

Peter also waited for Jesus' permission to step out of the boat.

It's no different with us. If we want to do what God has called us to do, we usually want to do it as quickly and successfully as possible. In contrast, God often wants us to wait on him. By waiting, we learn to depend on him and learn valuable lessons about faith, prayer, obedience, and trust that can change our lives forever.

GROUP DISCUSSION

1. When we realize how big our God really is, how does that realization affect us in the following areas:

   a. Our view of ourselves?

   b. Our belief that we are what we do?

   c. Our hope for the future?

   d. Our courage in stepping out of the boat?

   e. Our ability to wait on God?

2. Why is learning to wait on God so important as we prepare to get out of the boat?

3. John Ortberg writes that "prayer allows us to wait without worry." What do you think he means?

4. How will what we've explored today influence your response to "waiting on God?"

PERSONAL JOURNEY

When we step out of the boat and walk with God, anything can happen. We may soar, but that's not the only way we walk with God. Isaiah 40:31 describes soaring, but it also describes running and not being weary and walking but not fainting. Although we might think that soaring is the only way to go, God might have a different idea. His purposes may require that we run or walk.

1. Which of the following verbs from Isaiah 40:31 best describes you in your walk with God right now?

   You're soaring. Things are great spiritually. You find yourself borne up by God's power. You are out of the boat. God is answering your prayers, using you in special ways. You are productive in your life's work and flooded with strength and wisdom beyond your ability.

   You're able to run and not be weary. Life is challenging, with few miracles. But you are running the race with persistence and determination. You feel stretched but also feel God's pleasure in your obedience. You continue to run—faithfully serving, obeying, giving, and praying.

   You're walking but not fainting. You are hanging on to God but don't seem to be fruitful or productive. You are hardly triumphant, but you won't let go. You keep obeying God and putting one foot in front of the other. You refuse to quit even though you stumble.

Walking with God Is More Than Soaring

Even Jesus didn't soar all the time. Consider what he experienced as he walked with God during his earthly life:

- *Soaring* (Matthew 17:1–9; John 11:38–44). Jesus was transfigured in front of Peter, James, and John and spoke with Moses and Elijah. Jesus also raised his friend Lazarus from the dead.
- *Running but not becoming weary* (Matthew 16:5–11; Mark 3:4–7; Luke 19:41–44). Jesus was frustrated by the slowness of his disciples, he faced great opposition from the religious leaders of his day, he wept over the defiance of Jerusalem, but he kept on running. Relentlessly he pursued God's calling.
- *Walking and not growing faint* (Matthew 27:27–35). Jesus wasn't running when they put the cross on his bruised and bleeding back. He stumbled and fell as he walked, so another man had to carry his cross. Life was hard for Jesus, but he refused to quit. He kept on walking — to the cross, for us.

---

2. Considering where you are right now, what does the next step out of the boat look like for you?

3. Just as John Ortberg asked participants in the video to write down the word or phrase that keeps them from getting out of the boat, each of us needs to do the same. On the boat illustration on page 111, write out what keeps you in the boat.

When you are ready to let go of what is keeping you in the boat, tear the boat out of this book and burn it or throw it away.

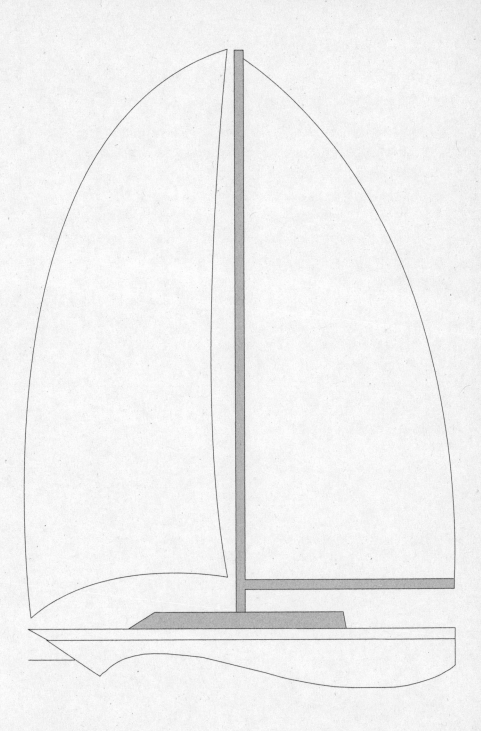

4. Think about how your life is going right now in terms of stepping out of the boat.

   a. In what areas do you need to rediscover God's greatness and trust him?

   b. What temptations are you facing that, if acted on, would be quite contrary to waiting on and trusting God?

   c. In what areas do you find it hard to hope?

   d. Is this a time when you need to act or wait on God? Why?

   e. When are you going to take that next step?

We each have the opportunity of a lifetime to get out of the boat and walk with God. No matter how much we know about God, or how much we have experienced with him, getting out of the boat is still a big step. There's always risk and the possibility of failure, but it's the only way we'll ever get to soar!

·O·TC OLD TESTAMENT CHALLENGE

Help your congregation experience the life-changing relevance of the Old Testament

The Old Testament Challenge (OTC) is a turn-key program to help everyone in your church understand and apply the Old Testament. Participants experience the content in multiple contexts: through sermons, group discussions, and personal devotions.

This 32-week series is designed for churches to teach, study, and discuss the entire Old Testament over a 9-month period. The goal of OTC is to discover the life-changing truths of the Old Testament and how they can be applied to daily life. Based on Pastor John Ortberg's OTC series at the New Community services of Willow Creek Community Church, this resource enables churches to raise the level of biblical literacy and understanding among their congregations. Your congregation will fall in love with the Old Testament!

The OTC curriculum is made up of 4 kits of 7-9 lessons each. This first kit covers the Pentateuch and includes everything you need to preach 9 sermons (that's less than $25 per week!):

- Teaching Guide containing material from Ortberg's weekly teachings for pastors and/or teachers
- Group Discussion Guide focusing on specific passages from the Old Testament designed for weekly or bi-weekly use and including leader's notes
- DVD and VHS Video presenting an OTC "vision-casting" message from Ortberg, a promotional piece for churches, and 4 creative video elements for each kit to use during the OTC message
- CD-ROM providing 7-9 PowerPoint® presentations for use with each of the OTC messages. It also contains 40 FAQ sheets answering tough questions from the Old Testament for use on your web site or to be printed in hard copy.
- Sets of slides for each teaching session for pastors and teachers
- Sermon Audio CD set containing all 9 messages preached by John Ortberg
- Implementation Guide
- *Taking the Old Testament Challenge* reading guide

Old Testament Challenge –Kit 1
ISBN: 0-310-24891-4

Old Testament Challenge –Kit 2
ISBN: 0-310-24931-7

Old Testament Challenge –Kit 3
ISBN: 0-310-25031-5

Old Testament Challenge –Kit 4
ISBN: 0-310-25142-7

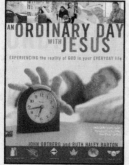

GRACE. JOY. FREEDOM
Good $ense

Transformational Stewardship for Today's Church

Are these the first words that come to mind when you think of stewardship? They could be! These are the words that people most often use to describe *Good $ense*—a field-tested, proven resource for changing hearts and lives in the area of finances.

Based on over sixteen years of ministry at Willow Creek Community Church, *Good $ense* by Dick Towner and the Good $ense Ministry team of Willow Creek includes resources designed to train and equip church leaders, volunteer counselors, and everyone in church.

- Church leaders –*The Good $ense Implementation Guide* and fifteen-minute *Casting a Vision for Good $ense* video equip church leaders to launch and lead a year-round stewardship ministry.
- Volunteer counselors –*The Good $ense Counselor Training Workshop Leader's Guide*, *Participant's Guide* and *Manual*, sixty-five minute video, and PowerPoint® CD-ROM train volunteers to become Good $ense budget counselors.
- Everyone in your church –*The Good $ense Budget Course Leader's Guide*, *Participant's Guide*, forty-five minute video, and PowerPoint® CD-ROM train every believer—not just those in financial difficulty—to integrate biblical principles into their lives both financially and spiritually.

At last, a resource that provides practical tools to address the challenging topic of finances in a grace-filled, life-giving way—a way that makes Good $ense.

Curriculum Kit
ISBN: 0-7441-3724-1

Implementation Guide
ISBN: 0-7441-3725-X

Vision Video VHS
ISBN: 0-7441-3726-8

Budget Course Leader's Guide
ISBN: 0-7441-3727-6

Budget Course Participant's Guide
ISBN: 0-7441-3728-4

Budget Course Video VHS
ISBN: 0-7441-3729-2

Budget Course PowerPoint® CD-Rom
ISBN: 0-7441-3730-6

Counselor Training Workshop Leader's Guide
ISBN: 0-7441-3731-4

Counselor Training Workshop Participant's Guide and Manual
ISBN: 0-7441-3732-2

Counselor Training Workshop Video VHS
ISBN: 0-7441-3733-0

Counselor Training Workshop PowerPoint® CD-Rom
ISBN: 0-7441-3734-9

Normal? Who's Normal?

Everybody's Normal Till You Get to Know Them

John Ortberg

Not you, that's for sure! No one you've ever met, either. None of us are normal according to God's definition, and the closer we get to each other, the plainer that becomes.

Yet for all our quirks, sins, and jagged edges, we need each other. Community is more than just a word—it is one of our most fundamental requirements. So how do flawed, abnormal people such as ourselves master the forces that can drive us apart and come together in the life-changing relationships God designed us for?

In *Everybody's Normal Till You Get to Know Them*, teacher and best-selling author John Ortberg zooms in on the things that make community tick. You'll get a thought-provoking look at God's heart, at others, and at yourself. Even better, you'll gain wisdom and tools for drawing closer to others in powerful, impactful ways. With humor, insight, and a gift for storytelling, Ortberg shows how community pays tremendous dividends in happiness, health, support, and growth. It's where all of us weird, unwieldly people encounter God's love in tangible ways and discover the transforming power of being loved, accepted, and valued just the way we are.

Hardcover 0-310-22864-6
Unabridged Audio Pages® CD 0-310-25083-8
Unabridged Audio Pages® Cassette 0-310-25082-X

Pick up a copy today at your favorite bookstore!

ZONDERVAN™

GRAND RAPIDS, MICHIGAN 49530 USA
WWW.ZONDERVAN.COM

THE LIFE YOU'VE ALWAYS WANTED

Spiritual Disciplines for Ordinary People

JOHN ORTBERG

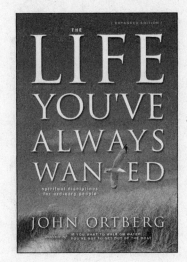

What does true spiritual life really look like? What keeps you from living such a life? What can you do to pursue it? If you're tired of the status quo—if you suspect that there is more to Christianity than what you've experienced—John Ortberg points to a road of transformation and spiritual vigor that anyone can take. It is the road that leads to *The Life You've Always Wanted*.

The Christian life is about more than being forgiven, more even than making it to heaven. John Ortberg calls us back to the dynamic heart of Christianity—God's power to bring change and growth—and shows us how we can attain it . . . and why we should attain it. *The Life You've Always Wanted* offers modern perspectives on the ancient path of the spiritual disciplines. Ortberg shows us that Christianity isn't a matter of externals, of outer form that gets the church stamp of approval, but of Christ's character becoming etched with ever-increasing depth into our own character.

As with a marathon runner, the secret lies not in trying harder, but in training consistently. Hence the spiritual disciplines. They're neither taskmasters nor an end in themselves. They're exercises that strengthen our endurance race down the road of growth. As we continue down that road, we'll see the signposts of joy, peace, and kindness, and all the hallmarks of a faith that's vital, real, and growing.

Paved with humor and sparkling anecdotes, *The Life You've Always Wanted* is an encouraging and challenging approach to a Christian life that's worth living. Life on the edge that fills our ordinary world with new meaning, hope, change, and a joyous, growing closeness to Christ.

Hardcover 0-310-24695-4
Unabridged Audio Pages® CD 0-310-24805-1
Unabridged Audio Pages® Cassette 0-310-24806-X

Pick up a copy today at your favorite bookstore!

GRAND RAPIDS, MICHIGAN 49530 USA

WWW.ZONDERVAN.COM

LOVE BEYOND REASON

Moving God's Love from Your Head to Your Heart

JOHN ORTBERG

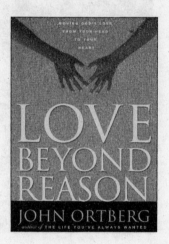

"Pandy" was only a child's rag doll—one arm missing, the stuffing pulled out of her. But in the eyes of the small girl who loved her, she was priceless.

In *Love Beyond Reason*, John Ortberg reveals the God you've longed to encounter—a Father head-over-heels in love with you, his child, and intensely committed to your highest joy. Ortberg takes you to the very core of God's being to discover a burning, passionate love that gives, and gives, and gives. He explores the life-changing ways this love has expressed itself through Jesus. And he shows how you, like Jesus, can love your mate, your family, your friends, and the world around you with the same practical transforming love.

Using powerful and moving illustrations Ortberg demonstrates the different characteristics of love—how it ...

- hears the heart
- delights in giving second chances
- balances gentleness and firmness
- chooses the beloved
- touches the untouchable
- teaches with wisdom
- walks in grace
- searches for those in hiding

... and walks in the kind of humility that, in the person of Jesus, willingly descended from the heights to don the rags of our rag-doll humanity.

John Ortberg pulls back the curtains of misconception to reveal what you've always hoped and always known had to be true; God's love really is a *Love Beyond Reason*. And it's waiting to flood your life with a grace that can transform you and those around you.

Hardcover 0-310-21215-4
Softcover 0-310-23449-2

Pick up a copy today at your favorite bookstore!

GRAND RAPIDS, MICHIGAN 49530 USA

WWW.ZONDERVAN.COM

WILLOW
Willow Creek Association

Willow Creek Association
Vision, Training, Resources for Prevailing Churches

This resource was created to serve you and to help you build a local church that prevails. It is just one of many ministry tools that are part of the Willow Creek Resources® line, published by the Willow Creek Association together with Zondervan.

The Willow Creek Association (WCA) was created in 1992 to serve a rapidly growing number of churches from across the denominational spectrum that are committed to helping unchurched people become fully devoted followers of Christ. Membership in the WCA now numbers over 10,000 Member Churches worldwide from more than ninety denominations.

The Willow Creek Association links like-minded Christian leaders with each other and with strategic vision, training, and resources in order to help them build prevailing churches designed to reach their redemptive potential. Here are some of the ways the WCA does that.

- **Prevailing Church Conference**—an annual two-and-a-half day event, held at Willow Creek Community Church in South Barrington, Illinois, to help pioneering church leaders raise up a volunteer core while discovering new and innovative ways to build prevailing churches that reach unchurched people.

- **Leadership Summit**—a once-a-year, two-and-a-half-day conference to envision and equip Christians with leadership gifts and responsibilities. Presented live at Willow Creek as well as via satellite broadcast to over sixty locations across North America, this event is designed to increase the leadership effectiveness of pastors, ministry staff, volunteer church leaders, and Christians in the marketplace.

- **Ministry-Specific Conferences**—throughout each year the WCA hosts a variety of conferences and training events—both at Willow Creek's main campus and offsite, across the U.S. and around the world—targeting church leaders in ministry-specific areas such as: evangelism, the arts, children, students, small groups, preaching and teaching, spiritual formation, spiritual gifts, raising up resources, etc.

- **Willow Creek Resources®**—to provide churches with trusted and field-tested ministry resources in such areas as leadership, evangelism, spiritual formation, spiritual gifts, small groups, stewardship, student ministry, children's ministry, the use of the arts—drama, media, contemporary music—and more. For additional information about Willow Creek Resources® call the Customer Service Center at 800-570-9812. Outside the U.S. call 847-765-0070.

- *WillowNet*—the WCA's Internet resource service, which provides access to hundreds of transcripts of Willow Creek messages, drama scripts, songs, videos, and multimedia tools. The system allows users to sort through these elements and download them for a fee. Visit us online at www.willowcreek.com.

- *WCA News*—a quarterly publication to inform you of the latest trends, resources, and information on WCA events from around the world.

- *Defining Moments*—a monthly audio journal for church leaders featuring Bill Hybels and other Christian leaders discussing probing issues to help you discover biblical principles and transferable strategies to maximize your church's redemptive potential.

- *The Exchange*—our online classified ads service to assist churches in recruiting key staff for ministry positions.

- **Member Benefits**—includes substantial discounts to WCA training events, a 20 percent discount on all Willow Creek Resources®, access to a Members-Only section on WillowNet, monthly communications, and more. Member Churches also receive special discounts and premier services through WCA's growing number of ministry partners—Select Service Providers.

For specific information about WCA membership, upcoming conferences, and other ministry services contact:

Willow Creek Association
P.O. Box 3188, Barrington, IL 60011-3188
Phone: 847-570-9812
Fax: 847-765-5046
www.willowcreek.com

We want to hear from you. Please send your comments about this book to us in care of zreview@zondervan.com. Thank you.

GRAND RAPIDS, MICHIGAN 49530 USA

WWW.ZONDERVAN.COM